40 DAYS THROUGH ADVENT WITH METROPLEX

CONTENTS

Introduction to the Advent Season

Pre-Advent:

Day One: *The Now and the Not Yet* by Josh Wright

Day Two: *God Can Use You and Me as Messengers* by Koshy Muthalaly

Day Three: *Be Ready to Honor God* by Steve Schneider

Advent Week One: Hope

Day Four: *Hope's Crumbs* by Josh Wright

Day Five: *Hoping for a Shepherd to Save Us* by Brooke and Daniel Brantley

Day Six: *Beautiful Feet* by BJ Keeter

Day Seven: *Desperate Hope is Still Hope* by Josh Wright

Day Eight: *Not the Present I Asked for* by Blake Mohling

Day Nine: *Jesus: God's Hope for Our Future* by Kathleen O'Connor

Day Ten: *For Unto Us a Child is Born* by Rob Thorson

METROPLEX CHURCH OF THE NAZARENE

Advent Week Two: Peace

Day Eleven: *Shalom* by Josh Wright

Day Twelve: *It Is Well with My Soul* by Janice Graves

Day Thirteen: *God's Peace in Us* by Dick Bergland

Day Fourteen: *His Peace Remains* by Selena Kyzer

Day Fifteen: *Prince of Peace* by James R. Russom DMin. NBC Faculty Emeritus

Day Sixteen: *Peace Comes at the Right Time* by Jeff Liles

Day Seventeen: *How Do You Describe Peace?* by Rob Thorson

Advent Week Three: Joy

Day Eighteen: *O Christmas Tree* by Erica Bingham

Day Nineteen: *Good News of Great Joy for All People* by Andrew Marston

Day Twenty: *Excitement and Fear Mixed with Joy* by Rob Thorson

Day Twenty-One: *The Joy of God's Comfort* by Josh Wright

Day Twenty-Two: *The Joy of Jesus' Birth* by Becki Sipes

Day Twenty-Three: *Abundant Joy* by James R. Russom DMin. NBC Faculty Emeritus

Day Twenty-Four: *Bundles of Joy* by Nathan Bingham

Advent Week Four: Love

Day Twenty-Five: *We Love Because We Are Loved* by Jennifer Bergland

Day Twenty-Six: *Love in Action* by Ashley Agee

Day Twenty-Seven: *Children of the Family Business* by Patrick Moore

Day Twenty-Eight: *The Love of God Too Big for Words* by Josh Wright

Day Twenty-Nine: *Meanings of Love* by Rex Dorough

Day Thirty: *Love is Out There* by Dick Bergland

Day Thirty-One: *God's Gift of Love* by James R. Russom, DMin. NBC Faculty Emeritus

Post-Advent: Two Days Before Christmas to New Year's Eve

Day Thirty-Two: *Christmas a Humbug?* by Josh Wright

Day Thirty-Three: *Sacred Stew and Cornbread* by Jennifer Bergland

Day Thirty-Four: *A Star and a Promise* by Kylee Lane

Day Thirty-Five: *Boxing Day* by Josh Wright

Day Thirty-Six: *Christmas for All* by Patrick Moore

Day Thirty-Seven: *What Do You Have to Give?* by Aimee BoJack

Day Thirty-Eight: *They Shall Call His Name Emmanuel* by Carole Liles

Day Thirty-Nine: *A Sword Will Pierce Your Own Soul* by Josh Wright

METROPLEX CHURCH OF THE NAZARENE

Day Forty: *The Gift That Keeps on Giving* by James R. Russom DMin. NBC Faculty Emeritus

Copyright © 2024 Metroplex Church of the Nazarene

All rights reserved.

All devotions are the intellectual property of their individual authors used with permission. No part of this book may be reproduced, or stored in a retrieval system, or transmitted in any form or by any means [electronic, mechanical, photocopying, recording, or otherwise] without express written permission of the publisher or the individual authors.

Edited by Josh Wright

Cover design by Mitchell Murrow

Scripture quotations marked (NIV) are taken from the Holy Bible, New International Version®, NIV®. Copyright © 1973, 1978, 1984, 2011 by Biblica, Inc.™ Used by permission of Zondervan. All rights reserved worldwide. www.zondervan.com The "NIV" and "New International Version" are trademarks registered in the United States Patent and Trademark Office by Biblica, Inc.™

Scripture quotations marked (NRSV) are taken from the New Revised Standard Version Bible, copyright 1989, Division of Christian Education of the National Council of the Churches of Christ in the United States of America. Used by permission. All rights reserved.

Scripture quotations marked (KJV) are taken from the King James Version of the bible.

Scripture quotations marked (NKJV) are taken from the New King James Version®. Copyright © 1982 by Thomas Nelson. Used by permission. All rights reserved.

Scripture quotations marked (NLT) are taken from the *Holy Bible*, New Living Translation, copyright ©1996, 2004, 2015 by Tyndale House Foundation. Used by permission of Tyndale House Publishers, Carol Stream, Illinois 60188. All rights reserved.

Scripture quotations marked ESV are from the ESV® Bible (The Holy Bible, English Standard Version®), © 2001 by Crossway, a publishing ministry of Good News Publishers. Used by permission. All rights reserved. The ESV text may not be quoted in any publication made available to the public by a Creative Commons license. The ESV may not be translated in whole or in part into any other language.

Lyrics to *O Come, O Come Emmanuel* translated by J.M. Neale

Lyrics to *Jesus Loves Me, This I Know* by Anna Bartlett

Warner

Lyrics to *It is Well with My Soul* by Horatio Spafford

"Hope" is the thing with feathers by Emily Dickinson

Lyrics to *The Love of God is Greater Far* by Frederick Martin Lehman

Original German Lyrics to *O Tannenbaum* by Ernst Anschütz

Lyrics to *Come Thou Long Expected Jesus* by Charles Wesley

Christmas Bells by Henry Wadsworth Longfellow

A Christmas Carol by Charles Dickens

INTRODUCTION TO ADVENT

If you're picking up this devotional and it's the first time you've ever celebrated the season of Advent: welcome! We're glad you've decided to spend the next forty days with us pouring over God's word as well as the songs of the church and poems from the hearts of our members celebrating this season so often overlooked. In the secular rhythms of the world, we often jump right into Christmas after Halloween and ride the wave of holly jolly joy all the way into the new year.

Advent is something the church has been doing for at least the last millennia and a half, though its exact origins are unknown. The word comes from the Latin *adventus*, meaning "coming" or "arrival." The Greek word is *parousia*, the word the early church would use to refer to the second coming of Christ. Different traditions revolve around the season, such as wreaths where candles are lit signifying various aspects of the anticipation of the season. Advent, at its heart, is a season of anticipation.

We look back to the Jews of Jesus' day, waiting for a Messiah. We contemplate the hope they had. We celebrate the joy Christ's coming would mean for the lowly and the disenfranchised. We long for the peace God's presence promises as our Emmanuel, God who is with us. We strive to embody the love that changed the world through a humble infant born to unknown parents in an insignificant corner of an empire the world thought might last forever.

But we also look forward. We hope for the day when Christ will come again. We long for the joy of our savior returning to set things right once again and order the world according to the peace that his presence brings into our chaos. We long for the love of God that will wipe every tear from our eyes in a world where death and pain will no longer hold sway.

Advent embraces the now and not yet nature of the kingdom of God, recognizing God's presence at work in the world around us while also knowing that this place is not our home. We rejoice, but we also wait. Things are not yet the way they have been and will be again when all of creation is reconciled unto its creator.

PRE-ADVENT

This devotional covers the 40 days at the end of the year. That means whatever year you're reading

this, start on November 22nd. If you're reading it the year the devotional was originally published (2024), that gives you three days of pre-Advent devotions before we begin reading about hope

on November 25th in the week leading up to the first Sunday of Advent. Advent is always the four Sundays before Christmas. The first Sunday of

Advent can be any day between November 27th and

December 3rd. If you're reading this some other year and are worried about the dates, or you're worried about keeping up with a daily devotional every day for forty days, don't be! Move through these devotions at your own pace and in your own way. May these words bless you whenever they find you, and may God speak to you through us.

DAY ONE

<u>The Now and The Not Yet</u>

By Josh Wright

*O come, O come, Emmanuel,
And ransom captive Israel;
That mourns in lonely exile here,
Until the Son of God appear.
Rejoice! Rejoice! Emmanuel
Shall come to thee, O Israel.*

—O Come, O Come Emmanuel

The Church has been singing these words for over a millennium. From monks chanting in Latin in ancient corridors all the way down to the twenty-first century, these words have resounded with hope. Not only the hope of a people two thousand years ago longing for a Messiah who came to be God in the flesh and show them a better way to The Father, but also the hope of his people who wait for a second coming in a world ravaged by sin and hate.

Advent bridges the gap between these two realities as we continue to live into the now and not yet kingdom.

Christ came. He came to be the light of hope dawning on those living in great darkness. He came to be our Prince of Peace. He came to proclaim joy in being falsely accused of evil for the sake of his kingdom. He came to show us the love of God: a love so great that not even death is too high a price to pay or too powerful an enemy to be overcome.

But Christ is also coming. He is coming to lift up every valley and bring every mountain low so that God's glory might be revealed, and all flesh might see it together. He is coming to reconcile the world back to God so that the divine shalom might reorder things according to The Father's will. He is coming to wipe every tear from our eyes and banish death and mourning and pain forever. He is coming to establish the love of God in the midst of the people of God at the restoration of all things.

Like Ancient Israel, we are captive still to sin and death in the pain of the here and now. Like Israel, we find ourselves living in exile; we are strangers in a strange land. But, like Israel, we can rejoice because Jesus is our Emmanuel, and he is coming.

Questions for Reflection:

1. What are you hoping for this Advent season? How do you think God might fulfill that hope?
2. Can you think of a time God showed up in your life in an unexpected way? What were you expecting to happen, and what

happened instead?
3. The term "shalom" is the Hebrew word for peace, but it's meaning is more like "things being reordered according to God's will." What can you do in your life this Advent season to reorder things to be more aligned with God's will?

DAY TWO

God Can Use You and Me as His Messengers!

By Koshy Muthalaly

Our God is sovereign, and He can do anything He wants in any way He wishes to do it. But the Bible reminds us that *"His ways are not our ways, nor our thoughts His thoughts."* (Isaiah 55:9, KJV)

Remember the last time you received some good news? A job offer, a promotion, an unexpected answer to prayer, the birth of a child? You were elated. Joy brought a smile to your face and a song to your heart. You wanted to trumpet it to the world! Our God works in some mysterious ways on behalf of His children. Good news can come in various ways. And Good News must be shared!

In the Christmas story, we see how God announces the Good News to the world. He chooses to do it through simple, ordinary shepherds at Bethlehem.

Shepherds were the lowest of the low in Jewish society. They made their living by raising smelly sheep. These men did not have membership in any city council. No one even knew their names. But God chose them to be the first to hear about the coming of the Messiah.

God often uses ordinary *"unlearned and ignorant men"* (See Acts 4:13, KJV) to fulfill His purposes. That is how Luke describes the disciples, but adds *"they took knowledge of them, that they had been with Jesus."* (Ibid.) When we encounter the Messiah in our hearts, we will be transformed. God seeks humility to serve His purposes. He wants others to see that we have "been with Jesus."

We are now the bearers of the Good News.

Questions for Reflection:

1. What does the fact that Jesus as Messiah came to bring the "Good News" mean to you?
2. How can you carry the Good News of Jesus today?
3. We all have our own "shepherds of Bethlehem." Who are the people you wouldn't expect to be bearers of God's Good News that God is still capable of working

through?

DAY THREE

<u>Be Ready to Honor God</u>

By Steve Schneider

After the Israelites crossed the river, God instructed the Israelites to select 12 men from the nation of Israel, one from each tribe. These representatives were each to carry a rock from the middle of the Jordan River. They were to select a rock from the spot where the priests stood holding the Ark of the Covenant in the middle of the river. After selecting a rock, they were to stack them in the location where they spent their first night after crossing the river.

That place came to be known as Gilgal. This was to be a memorial. This was their way of reflecting on God's blessings and to honor Him. They were to honor God by erecting a memorial consisting of the twelve stones.

The same principle is true for us. God expects us to honor Him with our lives. We honor Him by:

Worshipping Him publicly and privately. The word praise, which is another word for worship, comes from a Latin word meaning value or price. Therefore, to give praise to God is to proclaim His merit or worth.

We honor God as we take communion together. When we take communion we are proclaiming Jesus' death, burial, and resurrection.

We honor God as we follow the Lord in baptism. When we are baptized we proclaim the new life that Jesus has given us.

We honor the Lord by giving a tithe of our income. When we give our financial resources to God we are honoring Him. (Proverbs 3:9)

We honor the Lord by serving other people.

Honoring God is to emphasize that following God is a life process. Honoring God requires your life, not just a part of it or a corner of it.

Questions for Reflection:
1. What can you do this Advent season to honor God in your life?
2. Crossing the Jordan River was a significant moment in the life of The Israelites, marking their entrance into the promise land. Are things feeling significant to you

right now, or like every day is just like the day before it? What can you do to create more significance and intention in your days this Advent season?
3. Steve reminds us in this devotion that "honoring God requires your life, not just a part of it or a corner of it." Are there parts of your life you've been holding back from God?

ADVENT WEEK ONE: HOPE

Hope is not the same thing as optimism. Hope can stand firm even when everything about our circumstances suggests to us that things are not going to turn out the way we want. Hope anchors itself in our trust in the nature and character of God. In this week of Advent, we commit ourselves to the belief that God is in control and even when *"hate is strong and mocks the song of peace on earth, goodwill to men,"* *"God is not dead nor doth he sleep."*

DAY FOUR

<u>Hope's Crumbs</u>

By Josh Wright

"Hope is the thing with feathers
That perches in the soul
And sings the tune without the words
And never stops—at all,"
But I worry that, perhaps,
I've lost the ears to hear,
Because my tuneless humming
Has turned to anxious fear.

Hope may spring eternal,
But perhaps the well runs dry
When you lose the will to hope for more
Than barely getting by.
I've traded hope for certainty
In a life that's mostly fine:
I've clipped my wings, scorned finer things,
And swallowed my repine.

But I'm longing for something better
Like the passions I've forced myself to deny,
And ever since I clipped my wings
I've been dreaming about the sky.
If the song has never stopped
But you can't hear it ringing,
Instead of waiting for a musician
You should just start singing.

Questions for Reflection:

1. Have you gone through seasons where "hope's song" is hard to hear?
2. Are there times in your life where you settle for "good enough" instead of striving towards the things God's hope has promised? What can you do to reignite that hope this Advent season?
3. Is there something in your life you're hoping for that you've learned to live without instead?

DAY FIVE

Hoping for a Shepherd to Save Us

By Daniel and Brooke Brantley

Hear, O Shepherd of Israel, leading Joseph like a flock;
shine forth, you that are enthroned upon the cherubim.
In the presence of Ephraim, Benjamin, and Manasseh,
stir up your strength and come to help us.
Restore us, O God of hosts;
show the light of your countenance,
and we shall be saved.
O Lord God of hosts,
how long will you be angered
despite the prayers of your people?
You have fed them with the bread of tears;
you have given them bowls of tears to drink.
You have made us the derision of our neighbors,
and our enemies laugh us to scorn.
Restore us, O God of hosts;
show the light of your countenance,
and we shall be saved...

Let your hand be upon the man of your right hand,
the son of man you have made so strong for yourself.
And so will we never turn away from you;
give us life, that we may call upon your Name.
Restore us, O Lord God of hosts;
show the light of your countenance,
and we shall be saved.

(Psalm 80:1-7, 16-18, NRSV)

The words of this Psalm are not all positive, yet they are filled with hope. Despite the situation, the writer has such hope for what is to come. He has faith that God will deliver; faith that the hard times are not the end of the story.

It's easy in life to dwell on circumstances, focusing on the hard times or how alone we feel. We need to cling to the hope the psalmist has in these words, *"Restore us, O God of hosts; show the light of your countenance, and we shall be saved."*

God is in the restoration business. He never leaves us; He is always ready to save us. I love the Christmas season because it reminds us of that hope, and the fulfillment of that hope through Jesus.

Questions for Reflection:

1. Can you think of a time when you struggled to see the hope or light in a situation? How

did God reveal Himself to you in that time? Where did you find hope?
2. If you are in a space now where hope is hard to see, meditate on this passage. Be reminded that God hears our cries for mercy, peace, and hope.
3. During this season of Advent, what are you hoping for? Where do you see God showing up in new ways?

DAY SIX

<u>Beautiful Feet</u>

By BJ Keeter

*How beautiful upon the mountains
are the feet of the messenger who announces peace,
who brings good news,
who announces salvation,
who says to Zion, 'Your God reigns.'
Listen! Your sentinels lift up their voices,
together they sing for joy;
for in plain sight they see
the return of the LORD to Zion.
Break forth together into singing,
you ruins of Jerusalem;
for the LORD has comforted his people,
he has redeemed Jerusalem.
The LORD has bared his holy arm
before the eyes of all the nations;
and all the ends of the earth shall see
the salvation of our God.*

(Isaiah 52:7-10, NRSV)

Babylon conquered God's people, and Nebuchadnezzar took the best and the brightest from Judah and left the rest. The people wept and mourned because they were sure their future was over. But Isaiah 40 through 55 brings good news to a people in exile: God is going to release the captives and bring about salvation! But it's going to take some time. To prepare the way, they send a messenger ahead to Judah to tell them the captives have been released and they're coming back.

Sentinels who were set up in their towers to watch could tell when they saw the messenger still far off if the news would be good or not by their body language. "Beautiful feet" meant the messenger had happy body language; the messenger had joy because he had good news to share. So how beautiful on the mountains are the feet of one who brings good news! They began to celebrate and rejoice before the messenger even arrived! And they started to prepare for God's victory to enter in.

There is a pattern throughout Scripture that is similar to the pattern of our lives. There is a problem, we face struggle, tension, and bondage. But then a messenger comes announcing good news. And this good news brings about a new reality; it changes things. The question is: what are we going to do now? How are we going to live this out?

Whatever bondage you feel yourself entrapped in, Christ has come to set us all free. That's great news, but we have to respond!

Some of us have a long journey ahead of us to break bad habits. But the good news is they can be broken. Let's not just be hearers who rejoice in the good news, but also doers who respond and apply it. God can change our hearts and attitudes, but we have to submit ourselves to become followers, not just believers. Whatever bondage you are in, we have a God who hears us, knows us, and delivers us.

Lastly, look at your own feet for a moment. Are they beautiful? We're not only transformed by the good news; we're also called to be the messengers of this good news. Paul says "Ambassadors of reconciliation" in the world. So, how do you carry the Gospel of Jesus Christ? Does your relationship with lost people look, sound, and feel like good news to them? Do they rejoice when they see you approaching? Do you have joy because you have good news to share?

Lord I pray for some today who may find themselves in bondage to sin, to habits, or maybe even to the law. It can be difficult for us to trust and apply this wonderful "good news." May today be the day we respond to the good news you bring. May your grace and love win out and may your new creation get the last word in our lives. Give us beautiful feet, and may our lives reflect the good news we carry in Jesus' name. **Amen.**

Questions for Reflection:

1. How can you share the message of God's good news in your life this week?
2. Are there things in your life holding you back from being an ambassador of reconciliation? What can you do to bring good news to those living in bondage who need to hear about the hope they have in Christ?
3. What can you do to change the patterns in your life today and break the bondage of sin over you?

DAY SEVEN
<u>Desperate Hope is Still Hope</u>

By Josh Wright

I know that my redeemer lives,
and that in the end he will stand on the earth.
And after my skin has been destroyed,
yet in my flesh I will see God;
I myself will see him
with my own eyes—I, and not another.
How my heart yearns within me!

(Job 19:25-27, NIV)

Often we confuse (or at least conflate) hope and optimism. Optimism is believing that things will turn out good with little to no evidence or proof. Hope can be optimistic, but even after optimism fades we can still hold on desperately to hope.

Job had spent all his life believing in the goodness of God. He believed in his promises of blessing and goodness towards those who follow him and seek after him. In short order Job lost his children, his possessions, and his health. He spent a week in silence mourning for all he had lost, scratching at his oozing sores with broken shards of pottery.

Job's wife gave up hope. She told him to curse God and die. Even Job's friends were convinced that somehow Job had done something to deserve this calamity, clinging to the optimism of the belief that good things only happen to good people and bad things only happen to bad people.

Job no longer had optimism about his circumstances. He cursed the day of his birth, saying it would have been better to never have been born at all instead of enduring all this suffering. He lamented this calamity that had fallen on him without just cause. He was angry with God for his circumstances, but he still had hope.

Hope that God was still his redeemer. Hope that God would come to bring justice out of injustice, peace and order out of chaos and destruction. Hope that even if his very flesh rotted away he would still see in person the coming of the day of the Lord revealed to him and not another.

Optimism comes from a place of prediction or wish fulfillment; things have been good, so things will be good. Hope comes from a deep and abiding trust in the nature and character of God. God's people hoped for a Messiah because they believed in the goodness of God and his abiding faithfulness. Hope clings to that trust even when circumstances suggest we hope in vain, because hope is rooted deeper than merely wishing things will get better. Hope is rooted in the firm foundation of the nature and character of God.

Questions for Reflection:
1. Can you think of a time in your life when you had desperate hope? How did God show up? Was it different than you expected?
2. Is your hope merely optimism, or is it rooted in something deeper?

DAY EIGHT

Not The Present I Asked for

By Blake Mohling

I can still remember when I was a little kid watching the show *Family Matters*. One Christmas, I asked for a Steve Urkel talking pull-string doll that said some of the lines from the show. On Christmas morning, I remember eagerly opening presents looking forward to finding what I asked for. But I didn't get the Urkel doll that Christmas. Instead, I got an Urkel puzzle. Even though I've always loved puzzles, this was not the present I asked for, and I was kind of bummed.

When we think about Christmas, we think about the greatest present we could ever have received in Jesus Christ, but for many this was not the present/Messiah they asked for. They wanted a powerful ruler to restore the Kingdom to Israel. Instead, they got a humble servant who proclaimed the Kingdom of God. His power would not come through grand military gestures, but instead would come through the working of miracles and the love that He exemplified for us. I'm sure there were many like me on that first Christmas morning that were a little bummed to not get what they expected. They had no idea that they got something so much better.

So, sometimes we don't get exactly what we asked for at Christmas. But praise God that He gave us exactly what we needed in Christ's coming.

Questions for Reflection:

1. What was your favorite Christmas or birthday gift you received as a child? What (or who) made it so special?
2. Can you remember a time in your life when you didn't get what you wanted but wound up getting something you needed more instead?
3. It isn't always easy to trust God knows what we need better than we do. Is there something in your life that isn't going the way you planned? Do you think God might be doing something even better in that circumstance?

DAY NINE

Jesus: God's Hope for Our Future

By Kathleen O'Connor

Advent and the Christmas season may not be the time you necessarily think of human sinfulness and our need for a savior, but Jesus came into the world for a reason. God had closeness with human beings in the Garden of Eden, but it didn't take long for sin to enter the human race. But God knew all along what would happen. God knew and He planned for it. In Genesis 3:15 (NLT) we read God's first promise in the Bible:

> *"I will put enmity between you and the woman and He will crush your head."*

From the very beginning, God has been promising for his people redemption and salvation, and the promise of a Messiah points to that plan. Jesus was promised to be born of a woman. Jesus, God's promised gift for our future. Fast forward to John's Gospel, and we read:

> *"For God so loved the world that he gave his one and only Son, that whoever believes in him shall not perish but have eternal life. For God did not send his Son into the world to condemn the world, but to save the world through him." John 3:16-17 (NLT)*

As we open our gifts this year, let us remember that the reason for the season is not getting the newest toys or the nicest clothes. The best gift of Christmas is Jesus. He is God's promised hope for our future.

Father God, thank you for your gift of Jesus. I pray that in all the holiday hustle, that we would remember that Jesus is the best gift of all, God's promised hope for our future. **Amen**.

Questions for Reflection:

1. Are there times in your life you've seen God's actions after the fact that made it feel as though every step along the way was part of a plan you couldn't see?
2. God has always desired closeness with his children. How can you draw closer to

God this Advent season and live into the promises of the hope of Christ in our lives?

DAY TEN

For Unto Us a Child is Born

By Rob Thorson

*The people who walked in darkness
have seen a great light;
those who lived in a land of deep darkness—
on them light has shined.
You have multiplied the nation,
you have increased its joy;
they rejoice before you
as with joy at the harvest,
as people exult when dividing plunder.
For the yoke of their burden,
and the bar across their shoulders,
the rod of their oppressor,
you have broken as on the day of Midian.
For all the boots of the tramping warriors
and all the garments rolled in blood
shall be burned as fuel for the fire.
For a child has been born for us,
a son given to us;*

authority rests upon his shoulders;
and he is named
Wonderful Counselor, Mighty God,
Everlasting Father, Prince of Peace.
His authority shall grow continually,
and there shall be endless peace
for the throne of David and his kingdom.
He will establish and uphold it
with justice and with righteousness
from this time onwards and for evermore.
The zeal of the Lord of hosts will do this.

(Isaiah 9:2-7, NRSV)

I overheard my daughter reading from the eighth and ninth chapters of Isaiah a few days ago when I realized, once again, how much God loves His creation. So much so, He provided a way for His people to be reconciled back to Him out of the confusion and chaos of this world.

We serve a God who is, first of all, big enough to have created all things; big enough to fix all things. Isaiah chapter 8 leaves little to the imagination of how doomed and inclined to mass destruction God's people were and (at least partially) as a result of their own selfish attempts to manipulate life. Chapter 9 begins with a slight possibility of hope being introduced into this selfish world. As the chapter begins to resolve in verses 6-7, we are promised the hope of not only being redeemed, but also restored and reestablished by the God who created life itself; to bring us back under His wings of protection and promise of reconciliation.

The Hope God gives us is incredible, unbelievable, and immeasurable. We find our hope in the fact that somehow in God's being lives this beautiful thing called Love (because God is Love). Because of His Love, we have been given hope of a promised life of Love, not just in the chaos of the here and now, but also in the reconciled, restored life in Christ which prepares us for what is yet to come. Hope: it is what we set our eyes, hearts, and minds on in Christ.

Questions for Reflection:
1. Do you live in your day-to-day life as if God is big enough to fix all things, or do you try to fix things on your own more often than not?
2. What does the word reconciliation mean to you? When you hear the idea of God reconciling the world back to himself in Christ, what comes to your mind?
3. Have you set your eyes, heart, and mind on hope? If not, how can you choose to live more hopefully this Advent season?

ADVENT WEEK TWO: PEACE

The peace of God is so different than the way we often think about the word the two barely feel like synonyms. God does not settle for a pseudo-peace that is more lack of conflict than resolution of harm and reconciliation of parties who have been enemies. But neither does God seek to bring about peace through violence.

The people of Israel looked for a warrior king who would lead them in a military victory and restore the political glory of their ancestors. Instead, they received a humble and suffering servant, who declared blessings on the poor, the humble, the peaceful, and the broken.

The peace of God has the power to conquer, but what it most often conquers is our proud and haughty hearts.

DAY ELEVEN

Shalom

By Josh Wright

*The Lord bless you and keep you;
the Lord make his face to shine upon
you, and be gracious to you;
the Lord lift up his countenance upon
you, and give you peace.*

(Numbers 6:24-26, NRSV)

The peace of God is rooted in the word "*shalom*." *Shalom* is a Hebrew word that appears in the bible more than 170 times and is often translated as "peace." But *shalom* means more than just a lack of violence or a cessation of conflict.

God's peace is centered in right relationship with the divine and with the people around you. To say "peace be upon you" to a fellow Israelite was more than just wishing them a day free of chaos and difficulties to endure. It was telling them that your hope for their life was that it would be ordered exactly as God seeks it and that they would find themselves completely in-tune with the harmony of God's grace.

In the middle of explaining the role of the Holy Spirit's presence in the lives of his disciples, Jesus tells us in John's Gospel that his peace he leaves with us and gives to us. The indwelling presence of the Holy Spirit becomes our compass for following God's *shalom* in our lives. The Spirit guides us into the peace of God and keeps us on the path God has laid out for us.

And the indwelling presence of the Holy Spirit does not just bring a lack of violence and conflict. It brings us into the very presence and footsteps of God and directs us on how to live according to his will and purpose. The *shalom* of God's spirit at work in our lives fills us with his goodness and shows us his mercy, ordering our lives around his love.

Questions for Reflection:
1. What does peace mean to you? Where in your life do you most feel God's peace and presence?
2. How might seeking to walk in the will of

God day-by-day change your life? What's a good first step you can take right now down that path?

DAY TWELVE

It is Well with My Soul

By Janice Graves

*When peace like a river attendeth my way,
when sorrow like sea billows roll.
Whatever my lot...*

—It is Well with My Soul

We have all sung this beloved old song of the church. Or we have read the words of John 14:27 (NKJV) *"My peace I give to you; not as the world gives..."* These words have never been more real to me than this year.

There is peace when a loved one goes to heaven because you know they made it home, even though it leaves a big hole in your life. There is peace as you huddle in a storm shelter and whisper "not my will but thine" knowing you're in the path of an oncoming tornado. There is peace, too, when you realize God spared you and the hospital in its path.

We don't know what tomorrow has in store for us. All we know is that Christ wants us to trust that tomorrow to him as we follow him in complete obedience.

In this season of Advent, the Prince of Peace wants to fill us with his peace, the peace that can take us through the storms in our lives and protect us from harm. He is there. His peace is available. We need only ask. Praise God.

Questions for Reflection:
1. How has God's peace felt most present in your life lately? Where has it felt like God's peace was lacking?
2. What is the hardest thing about your "tomorrows" to surrender to God?
3. What's stopping you from asking for God's peace today?

DAY THIRTEEN

God's Peace in Us

By Dick Bergland

Peace is the state of tranquility, calm, or quiet. That sounds great but it also seems impossible to achieve. Job pressures, demands on our time, trying to keep up with what is expected of us—all these are problematic and push us further from real peace.

Jesus knew that human nature would not change unless there was a spiritual new birth within us. It's more than just inviting Christ into our hearts and living as Christians. It's about surrendering everything we are to the radical Lordship of Jesus Christ in our lives: daily, completely, and sacrificially.

Romans 5:1 (NIV) tells us, *"Therefore, being justified by faith, we have peace with God through our Lord Jesus Christ."* This peace *with* God is the type of peace we can have immediately. We can also have the peace *of* God. *"And the peace of God, which surpasses all understanding, will guard your hearts and minds through Christ Jesus."* (Philippians 4:7, NIV) And, we can have peace *in* God as it relates to the future.

Isaiah 9:6-7 (NIV) tells us that *"...His name will be called Wonderful, Counselor, Mighty God, Everlasting Father, Prince of Peace. Of the increase of His government and peace there will be no end."*

With God, *of* God, and *in* God. Find your state of tranquility, calm, and quiet in Him.

Questions for Reflection:

1. Do you find it harder to find peace *with* God, the peace *of* God, or peace *in* God? Why?
2. What keeps you from finding peace in your day-to-day life? What kind of changes could you make to better facilitate that peace?
3. Try to take at least five minutes out of your day this Advent season and seek the peace of God in your life.

DAY FOURTEEN

<u>His Peace Remains</u>

By Selena Kyzer

Peace I leave with you; My peace I give to you. Not as the world gives do I give to you. Let not your hearts be troubled, neither let them be afraid.

(John 14:27, NIV)

In the second week of Advent, we focus on peace. In John's Gospel, Jesus speaks to His disciples, offering them a gift of peace unlike anything the world can provide. Notice how He says, *"My peace I give to you."* This is not a generic peace or a fleeting feeling of calm; it is the very peace that Jesus Himself experienced. A peace rooted in His relationship with the Father. Jesus makes it clear that His peace is unlike the peace the world offers.

Worldly peace is often conditional and temporary, based on circumstances or external calm. It can disappear as quickly as it arrives, leaving us feeling unsettled. But the peace of Christ is steadfast and unchanging. It is not dependent on external situations but is anchored in the eternal reality of His love and care for us. His peace remains even when the storms of life rage because it is built on the solid foundation of God's unshakable promises.

Life was never promised without difficulty or uncertainty—whether it's personal challenges, global crises, or the weight of everyday responsibilities. Jesus doesn't dismiss these realities; He calls us to place our trust in Him. His peace is powerful enough to calm our anxious hearts. When we remember that Jesus is sovereign, we can face the unknown with confidence knowing we are never alone. And His peace is present *in* the trouble, a peace that carries us through the most difficult circumstances because it is grounded in His perfect love.

In a world still marked by conflict, division, and turmoil, we wait for the day when Christ will return and bring perfect peace to all creation. Be reminded that the peace Jesus offers is still available to us today, a peace that calms our fears and reassures our hearts, guiding and sustaining us.

Questions for Reflection:

1. Are there areas of your life where you are seeking peace from the world rather than from Christ?

2. What fears or anxieties can you surrender to Jesus today, trusting Him to replace them

with His peace?

3. How can you be a vessel of Christ's peace to those around you this Advent season?

Prayer:

Lord Jesus, thank You for the gift of Your peace, a peace that calms our hearts and stills our fears. Help us to remember that Your peace is not like the world's—it is steadfast, rooted in Your love and presence. As we walk through this Advent season, may we experience Your peace in deeper ways, and may we share that peace with others who are searching for hope and rest. We long for the day when You will return and bring perfect peace to all the earth. Until then, we place our trust in You. **Amen**.

DAY FIFTEEN

Prince of Peace

By James R. Russom, DMin.
NBC Faculty Emeritus

God's love is so inclusive! He did not reveal Christ only to the educated or persons of high stature, but also to common people like shepherds. The shepherds were tending their flocks when they were suddenly interrupted by angels bringing the Good News of the Messiah. This was such a surprise that they were both amazed and frightened. Like the shepherds, whose lives were interrupted by the unexpected, we too have frightening interruptions in life. When that happens, we can call on the Lord. And, in a glorious way, we discover that there is a deep settled peace in our souls in spite of the situation we are experiencing. But there is an important qualifier: God's peace comes to those *"on whom his favor rests."* (Luke 2:14, NIV) Good News! As the angel Gabriel said to Mary, *"you are blessed and highly favored."* (Luke 1:28, NIV) God's favor rests upon you because Jesus is your Savior.

When we are surprised by unexpected events, we react! Sometimes it is a positive surprise. But often these interruptions are negative. When they are negative and totally unexpected, we tend to lose any sense of joy and peace in our lives. But wait! God has a provision for that. It is Jesus, the Prince of Peace. Remember, Isaiah describes the Messiah as the *"Prince of Peace."* (Isaiah 9:6, NIV) This means that the peace that God the Father provides is given to us through His Son, Jesus.

We celebrate Advent amidst one of the most hectic seasons of the year. We get so busy preparing for the celebration of Christmas we tend to lose our sense of peace and joy. But beyond that are those times when we get surprises like: "You have cancer," or "Sorry, but we are going to have to let you go." What do we do then?

This is when we turn to Jesus. We lay our burdens at His feet and hear Him say, "Peace be with you." John describes three times when Jesus surprises his fearful and struggling disciples with these words. The word for peace here does not mean the absence of conflict or trouble. It is a state of being because of our right relationship with God through Christ. It is a peace that the storms of life cannot destroy.

So, if you are feeling harried, distressed, or facing an unexpected challenge, remember this: The Christ who came at Christmas is the Prince of Peace. Let Him flood your mind, heart, and soul with the peace of God that surpasses all understanding.

Questions for Reflection:

1. When was the last time you felt God's peace that passes all understanding?
2. Are you feeling favored by God right now? Why or why not?
3. What storms of life are you facing right now? How can God's peace help you today in weathering those storms?

DAY SIXTEEN

Peace Comes at The Right Time

By Jeff Liles

*Listen! It's the voice of someone shouting,
"Clear the way through the wilderness
for the Lord!
Make a straight highway through the wasteland
for our God!
Fill in the valleys,
and level the mountains and hills.
Straighten the curves,
and smooth out the rough places.
Then the glory of the Lord will be revealed,
and all people will see it together.
The Lord has spoken!"*

(Isaiah 40:3-5, NLT)

Peace is a result of God's presence. God does his great things in an order. Things need to happen in order for other things to happen, and not all of them might feel great at the time. But things from heaven don't happen by accident.

Listen! It's the voice of someone shouting. Have you ever stood next to someone as they were talking and not heard a word they said because your mind was somewhere else? Your mind was everywhere but there, so something will need to get your attention to focus on where you are right now.

Clear the way! Have you ever tried to go somewhere that you've never been, and the traffic is bumper to bumper? You question if there was a better way to go, or if the timing was not right, or maybe this was just not a place you should be going to.

Make a straight highway! Have you ever made a straight line on a wall then stepped back and realized the straight line was not very straight? Making something straight often needs a guide or measurement, or someone to take you from point A to point B.

Fill in! Have you ever had trouble filling in the blanks on a test? You studied and studied, and your mind suddenly went blank. Or maybe you tried to fill in a hole that seems impossible to fill.

Straighten and smooth! Have you ever tried to straighten out a hanger, or make a perfect circle with clay? It's a never-ending task with curving kinks and finger indents. Preparing the world for the coming of Jesus Christ, God's Son, was no easy task. Everything had to be right, even though so many things seemed to be wrong. God does not get in a hurry; God always plans ahead.

Jesus came to bring a new peace, a peace that had been forgotten. A peace that changes people. A peace that heals the soul.

Listen to the voice of the Holy Spirit. Clear out the things that interrupt your communication with God. Allow God to straighten the path in your spiritual journey. Fill your life with God's Love. Smooth out your relationships with God's Peace.

When things are right in you, the way God knows they need to be, God's Peace will wrap you up in a way that will change your life!

Questions for Reflection:
1. How do you discern the Holy Spirit's guidance in your life? Has God been directing you somewhere you've been reluctant to go?
2. Take 15 minutes today to listen to God. Quiet your mind and your heart, turn off the electronics and other distractions, and truly listen for God to speak to you.
3. Have you ever felt as if you knew God's goal for you but were unwilling to wait on God's timing? What do you do when you struggle to wait on God?

calling us.

Romans 13 reminds us to be subject to governing authorities because God is the author of authority, and nothing has been established without His sovereignty. We are also reminded in Isaiah that the government will be placed upon the shoulders of the One who will be called "Wonderful Counselor, Mighty God, Everlasting Father, and Prince of Peace." (Isaiah 9:6, NRSV) Jesus is that prince who will provide a peace without end.

Peace that is founded upon the originator of the very idea of peace: God Himself. God, who is bigger than anything, anyone, or any circumstance that this world has to offer, is the One from whom our peace is derived and always will be.

So, rest. Take heart in knowing that God in His love also provides peace. Find tranquility in knowing there will always be plenty of it to go around through your dark times and in your blessings. Shalom.

Questions for Reflection:

1. When you think about the word peace, what comes to mind?
2. Paul tells us in Romans 12:18 *"If it is possible, so far as it depends on you, live peaceably with all."* What do you do in situations where peace doesn't seem possible or depend on you?

3. How do we live at peace when our circumstances are anything but peaceful? How can we show God's peace to those living in darkness?

ADVENT WEEK THREE: JOY

The joy God brings does not come in spite of our circumstances; James tells us *"My brothers and sisters, whenever you face trials of any kind, consider it nothing but joy, because you know that the testing of your faith produces endurance; and let endurance have its full effect, so that you may be mature and complete, lacking in nothing."* (James 1:2-4, NRSV)

"Whenever you face trials of any kind, consider it nothing but joy" could more literally be rendered from the Greek as *"when troubles and adversity fall around you and surround you, let it lead you to joy."* The joy that comes from God is a choice, and it is forged in the crucible of our hardships not in the comfort and relaxation of our easiest days.

James tells us when we run into things that make us doubt our faith in Christ and his promises, we grow in maturity and learn how to stand strong and endure. God is a good Father, so he allows his children to struggle because he knows that struggling is how we become more like Christ.

DAY EIGHTEEN

O Christmas Tree

By Erica Bingham

O Christmas Tree, O Christmas Tree,
Your branches green delight us!
They are green when summer days are bright,
They are green when winter snow is white.
O Christmas Tree, O Christmas Tree,
Your branches green delight us!

When the holiday season approaches, there seem to be two teams. Both have very strong beliefs as to why they are right, and why the other team is wrong. You will likely even find yourself on one side or the other. I'm talking about, of course, whether you put up your Christmas tree before Thanksgiving or wait until after.

I used to be on "team wait." Then, one year I found myself facing unknowns like never before. The unknown often feels bleak and dark. So that year, in a moment of spontaneity, we put up our Christmas tree way before Thanksgiving. We started seeking light and joy both physically and spiritually. That year we put up our Christmas tree in October and it was so right and needed.

From that somewhat rash decision and break from tradition there was a daily reminder of the light that we live under. That Christ came as a light in the dark world and brought joy unspeakable. Now we have a new tradition where our Christmas tree always goes up early. Because, whether we think about it or not, the light of Christ is always shining, not just after Thanksgiving. So why not have our Christmas tree out early as a reminder…and maybe keep it out late, too!

Questions for Reflection:

1. Are you "team after" or "team before"? Are there any ways you can modify your routine/traditions to better highlight God's presence in your life?
2. Are your decorations just decorations or are they reminders of God's gifts?
3. Do your holiday traditions carry a special meaning about your relationship with God? Are there opportunities to use this as an avenue for sharing His love?

DAY NINETEEN

Good News of Great Joy for All People

By Andrew Marston

And there were shepherds living out in the fields nearby, keeping watch over their flocks at night. An angel of the Lord appeared to them, and the glory of the Lord shone around them, and they were terrified. But the angel said to them, 'Do not be afraid. I bring you good news that will cause great joy for all the people. Today in the town of David a Savior has been born to you; he is the Messiah, the Lord.'

(Luke 2:8-11, NIV)

The season of Advent is such a monumental time in the life of the Church and for followers of Christ. The message of Joy permeates throughout our communities of faith as we gather together each year in excited expectation for the arrival of the Messiah, Jesus.

Even for those outside of the Church, the theme of joy at Christmas takes center stage. TV commercials, internet ads, holiday specials, Christmas songs; in our world Christmas carries an inherent desire to manufacture joy. Christmas trees go up in our homes and presents go underneath. Companies plan office parties in order to boost morale. Retailers use ads to show all of the smiling faces of those who receive their products. And, for what feels like the 10,000th time, a girl from the big city falls in love with a small-town farmer on the Hallmark Channel. How could anyone not be joyful at Christmastime?

The reality is that for many (perhaps even some reading this short devotion), joy feels like the last thing that surrounds Christmastime. For some, declining health prevents participation in favorite traditions. Others can't afford presents this year. Maybe family gatherings have gotten smaller and only serve as a reminder of who's missing. Christmas is a joyful holiday...except when it isn't.

Maybe you find yourself lacking joy this holiday season. Maybe you're searching for a reason to celebrate. Luke Chapter 2 has good news for you: Christ has come into the world. This news first came to some shepherds out in a field. They played a part in society, but not one that would put them in any kind of high standing. And it was the middle of the night! They were alone and at that point, probably not the most joyful. But then came the news: the deliverer, the Messiah, had been born!

The coming of Jesus was good news of great joy for all people. This "all people" included those who did not have a reason to be joyful. In fact, it came *specifically* to them! This was a consistent theme for Jesus. He gave living water to the woman at the well. He wrote in the sand instead of casting stones at the woman caught in adultery. He raised Lazarus from the dead. He saw Zacchaeus when he was up in the tree trying to catch a glimpse. He gave blind beggars their sight. He freed Mary from demons.

Are you grieving? He'll wipe your tears. Are you lonely? He'll never leave you. Are you poor? He calls you blessed. Are you afraid? He gives you a Spirit of power, love, and sound mind. Are you forgotten? He sees, hears, and knows you. Today, right where you are, there is a Savior for you, and He is Christ the Lord!

Questions for Reflection:

1. Are you struggling to find joy at Christmastime this year? When you think about the people Christ came to bring good news to, do you find it hard to count yourself among them?
2. What does joy mean to you at Christmas?
3. Which of the stories about what Jesus did for people resonated most with you? Why?

DAY TWENTY

Excitement and Fear Mixed with Joy

By Rob Thorson

When the angels had left them and gone into heaven, the shepherds said to one another, 'Let us go now to Bethlehem and see this thing that has taken place, which the Lord has made known to us.' So they went with haste and found Mary and Joseph, and the child lying in the manger. When they saw this, they made known what had been told them about this child; and all who heard it were amazed at what the shepherds told them. But Mary treasured all these words and pondered them in her heart.

(Luke 2:15-19, NRSV)

"Do you think I have time to take a shower?" she asked standing in the doorway of the bathroom when her water broke.

Excitement and fear both flooded her soul as she realized it was time to give birth to her first child. But it would take more than excitement and fear to get through the next 16 hours of intense labor, achieving the intended result of what she had waited nine months for: a baby.

A baby. Helpless, dependent, selfish, difficult to communicate with. Yet, this baby brought joy that is overwhelming, fresh, and at times inexpressible. The joy birthed that day was undeniable. It went deeper than the pain of childbirth, the fear of the unknown, and the question of what to do next.

The joy that new life brings has an appeal like no other. Just watch the face of an elderly woman when a toddler waddles by. Or see the reaction of awe and wonder from a big brother or sister when a baby is placed in their arms. But none of these compare to the joy expressed from the very depth of the soul as a baby is held next to its mother's heart for the very first time.

The joy that Mary, the mother of Jesus, felt has been described as inexpressible, and as a father I get only a small measure in comparison to that feeling of joy. But remember, joy is more than a feeling. The good news given to Mary, Joseph, the shepherds, and eventually to the wise men from afar would also find its way into the hearts of everyone who believes in the name of Christ.

Joy, when properly absorbed, changes the very nature of a person. It goes beyond the realm of emotion into the reality of attitude. Because joy—true joy—comes only from our Creator.

It wasn't a silent night, but Joy was certainly in the air. The anticipation of what was to come was filling the hearts of those closest to the situation. Excitement and fear began to overwhelm a mother-to-be as she stood in the doorway of the bathroom in her home and asked whether she had time to take a shower as her water broke.

Questions for Reflection:
1. How has joy changed your life since Christ came into your heart?
2. What makes you feel the most joy? How often do you get to experience it?
3. When Mary was treasuring these things in her heart and pondering them, what do you think she was thinking and feeling? What would *you* be thinking and feeling?

DAY TWENTY-ONE

The Joy of God's Comfort

By Josh Wright

*Comfort, O comfort my people,
says your God.
Speak tenderly to Jerusalem,
and cry to her
that she has served her term,
that her penalty is paid,
that she has received from the Lord's hand
double for all her sins.*

(Isaiah 40:1-2, NRSV)

The joy of Advent comes through forgiveness. God's people knew of his power and might through the wondrous deeds he performed leading them out of Egypt and into the promise land. We saw the might of the Lord and heard about his desire for relationship with his people, but we were still no closer to God than we had been when we wandered east of Eden.

That lack of closeness led to the exile. God's people fell so short of God's will for so long, generation after generation, that destruction fell upon them. We lost our voice for praising and rejoicing, unsure of even how to sing the songs of the Lord in a strange land:

By the rivers of Babylon—
there we sat down and there we wept
when we remembered Zion.
On the willows there
we hung up our harps.
For there our captors
asked us for songs,
and our tormentors asked for mirth, saying,
'Sing us one of the songs of Zion!'
How could we sing the Lord's song
in a foreign land?

(Psalm 137:1-4, NRSV)

After we hung our harps on the poplars and the silence fell, we wept for the destruction of what God had built in and among us. We looked at the ruins of the promised land and wondered whether our hearts would ever know joy again.

But, after that destruction, in the quiet of the desolation left behind Isaiah speaks these words. He proclaims to the people that God's punishment is no longer upon them and instead they will see the glory of the Lord coming to be revealed in their lives.

METROPLEX CHURCH OF THE NAZARENE

We rejoice that God chose to pay the penalty for our transgressions with his own blood, and the hope of that reconciliation begins with the incarnation. It is to our great joy that Jesus came not only to bring comfort, but to be the comforting presence of God in our midst.

Questions for Reflection:

1. Is there a moment in your life God's forgiveness felt the most real? What was it?
2. What does it mean for you personally for Jesus to be Emmanuel and be God in the flesh with us?
3. Are there times or places in your life it feels hardest to be close to God? Reflect on what it is that makes God feel distant in those moments and how you can draw closer to him to make those moments feel less distant.

DAY TWENTY-TWO

The Joy of Jesus' Birth

By Becki Sipes

"All who heard it wondered at the things which were spoken to them by the shepherds. But Mary kept all these sayings, pondering them in her heart."

(Luke 2:18-19, ESV)

What Joy can be brought to our hearts when we think of a child's birth! Kissing little fingers and toes, giggling at the faces they make and snuggles; oh, the snuggles! Parents always want the best for this new gift of God. Enough food and milk. Enough protection. Enough diapers!

Mary wanted all these things for her first-born son. But her son would turn out to be much more than she expected. What if you were told that your son is an emissary from God? What if you realize that he is special because he understands Scripture better than religious leaders at the age of twelve? What if, as a young man, he can perform miracles? What if, instead of being a carpenter like his dad, he wanders the countryside gathering fishermen and tax collectors to follow him?

Jesus was extraordinary by human standards, but he was so much more. Jesus was sent to us to give new meaning to life. He sweat drops of blood so we could have a hope of peace that had never been dreamed of before. What other god would do something like this to give humanity a better life?

My Jesus was born in Joy and has spread Joy ever since. Join me in enjoying his leading, teaching, and miraculous future.

Questions for Reflection:

1. How do you think Mary and Joseph handled being the parent to such an extraordinary child? How do you think *you* would handle it?
2. What joy has Jesus spread in your life lately? What joy do you need him to bring?

DAY TWENTY-THREE

Abundant Joy!

By James R. Russom, DMin.
NBC Faculty Emeritus

JOY! We sing about it. We see it on decorations, written in Christmas cards, and taught during Advent. It is one of the most blessed aspects of our anticipation of what Christ will bring to the world. Joy is not a feeling, but a state of being; the result of living in right relationship with God in Christ. When the Spirit of God resides in our hearts by faith, we are changed. Love, joy, and peace are placed within our hearts. These Christlike characteristics enable us to live joyful lives.

The sages from the East were searching for a Promised King who would make a difference in the world. They followed the trail of a star in the sky; a sign that the King had come. In scripture it says:

"When they saw the star, they rejoiced with exceeding great joy." (Matthew 2:10, KJV) Joy beyond measure! The King has come at last!

Joy is given to us to experience as a way of life. We are enabled to face every life experience with a joy that the world did not give, nor can it take it away. It is not dependent upon circumstances. It is the result of the Spirit of Christ dwelling in our hearts. After telling them about the Father's love for him and the fruit they would bear if they abided in him, Jesus told his disciples: *"I have told you this so that my joy may be in you and that your joy may be complete."* (John 15:11, NIV) The word translated "complete" means "full to the brim and running over." It is like the "exceeding great joy" the wise men discovered because the king had arrived!

What does it mean to rejoice? It means to show great delight regarding something or someone. Isaiah was full of joy and found great delight in serving the God who clothed him in garments of salvation and righteousness and adorned his head like a priest or a bride and groom adorned with jewels representing their love for one another. If you have allowed Jesus to be Lord of your life you have great reason to be filled with rejoicing.

Advent is a time for us to rejoice. The King has come. He has blessed us with salvation, love, and joy. He has clothed us in righteousness. Now, let your joy be evident to all, for the King is as near to you as the air you breathe. Therefore, there is no reason to live with anxiety and fear. Live in the joy of the Lord!

Questions for Reflection:

1. When you see the word joy, what does it mean to you?
2. Are there times in your life you still live with anxiety and fear, even though God and his joy are near? What can you do to help you live in the joy of the Lord instead?
3. How do you feel about the idea of joy not being "dependent on circumstances?" Are there times in your life you feel like your joy changes because of what's happening around you?

DAY TWENTY-FOUR

<u>Bundles of Joy</u>

By Nathan Bingham

"In those days Caesar Augustus issued a decree that a census should be taken of the entire Roman world. (This was the first census that took place while Quirinius was governor of Syria.) And everyone went to their own town to register.

So Joseph also went up from the town of Nazareth in Galilee to Judea, to Bethlehem the town of David, because he belonged to the house and line of David. He went there to register with Mary, who was pledged to be married to him and was expecting a child."

(Luke 2:1-5, NIV)

While we face one of the most divisive election cycles in recent U.S. history it is regretful to read that the government was in the business of making life difficult for people even two thousand years ago. In the Gospel of Luke the story of Christ's birth, the story of Christmas, starts with a disruptive political decree. We do not read anything about Mary and Joseph's emotional response. No complaint about their travel or mislaid plans. Instead, this momentous and disruptive political scene is relegated to a minor backdrop in the Christmas story.

With a baby on the way, we find the new parents adjusting to any and all changes as their lives are now revolving around their soon-to-be born son. A son that we know was to be the savior of a chaotic world. As Christians, our lives too must revolve around this baby. So too must our lives reflect the importance of being centered around Christ.

While others may find the tumultuous waters of the world to be overwhelming, we are able to daily rejoice in the living God. The world does try to steal our joy with a constant stream of negative or polarizing media, but Christians stay focused on what is really important. Christmas is a joyful time when we can find the story of Christ referenced even in the secular world and we can use that redirection to help orient ourselves back towards our true center.

Questions for Reflection:

1. In what ways do you find yourself being pulled away from a Christ-centered focus in your daily life?
2. The parents of newborns change their whole schedule, lose tons of sleep, and can't stop talking about their new baby. Do you let Christ rule your life that way, or is he regulated to only 'church time'?
3. What are some ways that you can change your daily surroundings and interactions to help redirect your focus back toward Christ even when not in the traditional Christmas season?

ADVENT WEEK FOUR: LOVE

Love is a central theme in Scripture. The self-sacrificial love of God in sending us his son and Jesus' love in being willing to die for us are the lifeblood of our faith. But love also has to be expressed and lived out in the everyday and the mundane. It must be reflected in the way we treat each other, picking up our crosses day after day to follow the example of Christ. We are called to love the people we'd rather hate and to remember to treat everyone as if they were Christ himself.

DAY TWENTY-FIVE

We Love Because We Are Loved

By Jennifer Bergland

God's love was revealed among us in this way: God sent his only Son into the world so that we might live through him. In this is love, not that we loved God but that he loved us and sent his Son to be the atoning sacrifice for our sins. Beloved, since God loved us so much, we also ought to love one another. No one has ever seen God; if we love one another, God lives in us, and his love is perfected in us.

(1 John 4:9-12, NRSV)

As soon as I saw her, I knew I loved her. It was overwhelming. She was my first child, and I was unprepared for the intensity of this emotion. I didn't know what she would become or whether she would be easy or hard to raise. Those were details we'd figure out as her life unfolded. But in that moment, I instantly adored this little human.

Throughout Scripture, God reminds us that love is His idea—it's a God-given reality. This passage reveals that God showed His love by sending His Son into the world. This was His way of demonstrating how much He loves us. The prophet Isaiah called Him Emmanuel, which means God with us.

My love for my children, husband, and friends is only possible because God first loved me. He loved me enough to send His Son to be the atoning sacrifice for my sins.

You may be thinking, Jennifer... you're getting ahead of yourself. This is Christmas, not Easter! And yes, that's true, but we can rejoice at Christmas knowing Easter is coming. God loved us so that we can love others, and when we do, God lives in us and His love is perfected in us. There's a lot of good news in that sentence!

Questions for Reflection:
1. How has God's love shown you how to love? Are there people in your life you would struggle to love without God's help?
2. Have you ever been overwhelmed by love before? What caused that feeling?

3. Often we try to earn God's love rather than accepting it. Are there ways in your life right now you're trying to earn God's love?

DAY TWENTY-SIX

Love in Action

By Ashley Agee

How beautiful on the mountains are the feet of those who bring good news, who proclaim peace, who bring good tidings, who proclaim salvation, who say to Zion, 'Your God reigns!'

(Isaiah 52:7, NIV)

This past year I had the privilege to go on my first medical mission trip. I was able to travel with a team to a rural area of Panama and set up a clinic where we provided medical services free of charge for four days. I was excited to care for patients, but I admit I was skeptical about how much impact my efforts could have with such limited resources. I was looking at the problem through *my* eyes, not God's.

Once in Panama and working in the makeshift clinics, I realized the most important thing we ended up bringing to the people of Panama wasn't free supplies and medicine: it was the news of Jesus Christ. It was the message of love not only in our words, but in our actions. Each person who came through our clinic was seen first by our prayer team. Needs were prayed for, the gospel was shared, and Bibles in Spanish were available for anyone who wanted one. We were able to address some of the physical needs of the community. But, more importantly, we were also able to minister to the emotional and spiritual needs of the community.

Throughout the week I spent there, all that we gave of ourselves was given back to us. We ended our last clinic by singing a worship song with the members of the local church. Parts of the song were in English, and parts of the song we sang in Spanish. It was a beautiful portrayal of the global community of believers worshipping the same God, with the same message of love that started so many years ago when God sent his son to earth. A love that was not only spoken in words but lived out in the way Jesus met needs anywhere he found them: physical infirmities *and* spiritual ones.

Questions for Reflection:

1. Have you ever had any cross-cultural experiences that have helped you better understand the way people in another part of the world live? If so, how did it change

the way you live your life?
2. Is God calling you to do more for others in another culture, even if that culture is across town instead of halfway around the world? How can you make a bigger impact for the kingdom, locally and globally?

DAY TWENTY-SEVEN

Children of the Family Business

By Patrick Moore

Born Thy people to deliver, Born a child and yet a King, Born to reign in us forever, Now Thy gracious kingdom bring.

—Come, Thou Long Expected Jesus

I am in a season of transition, moving into a new phase of my career. Though I'm changing locations and creating my own counseling business, I'm reminded that I'm always in the Family Business of God. I feel God orchestrating events, working through His people. I seek His guidance in prayer and others are doing the same. Things are happening that some might call coincidental, but I trust God is in it. I can rest in His provision for me. I feel called to keep love and healing for the hurting at the center of my work as a counselor. At times I get anxious and impatient, and I have to remember to wait—wait on God.

As we wait in anticipation, we celebrate the coming arrival of Jesus into the world. We're in the last weeks of pregnancy, awaiting the birth of God Incarnate, coming incognito as a poor peasant baby. We already know His name: "God with Us." We wait with hopes and dreams, believing this child will set the world right. And we wait for His return, to finish what was started in us, always living in anticipation of God showing up, living with us, in us, and through us.

Watching and waiting for 2,000 years. Stay awake. The Kingdom is near. We are called to be the Kingdom today. If the world is liberated, it's because God has invaded the world through His children. We are in the family business of reconciling the world to Him.

We rely on the Father as the life in our lungs, the love flowing through our veins, all the good in the deeds of our hands and feet. With every act, we choose whose we are. When we embody the light, life, and love of the Great I AM, God moves in us and through us. We are Heaven's Kingdom becoming.

Jesus demonstrates the work we must do: to love

as He so loved the world, to serve as He served. We emulate Jesus so the world may know Him. He never left; we are His hands and feet, the Body of Christ. We're not here just to await His return. We're here to serve all our neighbors: the hurting, the lost, the homeless, immigrants, prisoners, prostitutes, politicians, bankers, tax collectors, the poor, and the rich. We must be willing to wash anyone's feet in the name of Jesus.

No one is untouchable. Everyone is invited to the Kingdom, and all of His children are called to join the family business: to bring everyone into the celebration of forgiveness, eternal life, and living love. This love flows from Love Himself, transforming lives and filling them to overflowing so they may bless others. We are called to transform the lives of anyone and everyone we encounter, just as He did.

This emulation is crucial: Jesus is God. Jesus walked among us as God's avatar, showing us that God is Love. Jesus is the embodiment of Love, and we too must embody Him as His emissaries. Jesus' message was simple: "Love God above all else, and love everyone else as if they were God." Whatever you do to others, you have done to God. I hear him saying, "I gave you the Spirit to carry on my work. Are you participating in the family business?"

Questions for Reflection:

1. How would it change our lives if we truly lived as though whatever we did to others, we have done to God?
2. Are there people in your life you treat as if they were "untouchable?" What are some steps you can take to change the way you think about that person or that group of people?
3. What can we do to be more patient as we wait on God? What can we do while we wait to be prepared for when God shows up to act?

DAY TWENTY-EIGHT

The Love of God Too Big for Words

By Josh Wright

I've always been intrigued by the ending verse of the Gospel of John:

> *"But there are also many other things that Jesus did; if every one of them were written down, I suppose that the world itself could not contain the books that would be written."*
>
> (John 21:25, NRSV)

Surely that's hyperbole? Even if we're including the years of his pre-ministry life, Jesus didn't make it to 40. John is telling us he did so much in those thirty some-odd years that the world doesn't have room for the books we could write about it?

It seems likely what John meant is something more akin to what Frederick Lehman wrote about the love of God:

> *Could we with ink the ocean fill,*
> *And were the skies of parchment made;*
> *Were every stalk on earth a quill,*
> *And every man a scribe by trade;*
> *To write the love of God above*
> *Would drain the ocean dry;*
> *Nor could the scroll contain the whole,*
> *Though stretched from sky to sky.*

The life of Jesus was so full of the love of God that we could write about it forever and run out of paper and ink. The life of Jesus so perfectly reflected the Father's love for us, his children, that any attempt to try and explain who Jesus is will fall short of experiencing Jesus for yourself and how powerful and life-changing the love of God he embodies is.

Questions for Reflection:
1. When you think about Jesus' love for you, what's the first thing that comes to mind? Why?
2. John's epistles tell us not only that God loves us, but that God *is* love. Why do you think

that attribute is the one John sees as most essential to God's nature?
3. Is there a place or time God's love feels most prevalent in your life? Why?

DAY TWENTY-NINE

Meanings of Love

By Rex Dorough

Love is expressed more during the Christmas season than any other time of the year.

There are so many things we love, and so many ways we love them. Love is the central theme of the Bible, especially in the New Testament. God is love: probably the greatest example of God's love is in John 3:16 (NIV). *"For God so loved the world, that he gave his one and only Son, so that whoever believes in him shall not perish but have eternal life."* Many other places in the Bible speak of God's love.

Ancient Greek, the language the New Testament was written in, speaks about four different types of love. *Eros* (romantic love) and *Storge* (love for family) don't appear specifically in the New Testament, but the concept of these types of love is found throughout the scriptures.

Philia is brotherly love, the love found in friendships. This Greek word describes the powerful bond among friends. This love is best found in churches that show how Christians should interact with one another. The Church should be known for the kind of love that centers around care, respect, compassion, and deep connections among each other.

Agape is the highest form of love: unconditional love that only God can give. This word shows God's immeasurable and incomprehensible love for us. *Agape* love is found perfectly in Jesus. With the help of the Holy Spirit, we should strive to experience and show this kind of love.

The thing all these types of love have in common is that they have to be accepted by a person before they can experience them.

Questions for Reflection:

1. The Bible doesn't just teach us about God's love, it challenges us to live in light of what He has done for us. Take some time to reflect on God's love for you and ask yourself: are you extending the same love to those around you?

2. How can you better express God's love towards others this Christmas season?
3. Are there places in your life where someone is trying to show love to you and you haven't accepted it? Why?

DAY THIRTY

Love is Out There

By Dick Bergland

Where is it? Am I supposed to be looking for it? Is it going to find me? What does it mean, that it is "out there?" Love is a huge word. It can involve so much and means so many different things. The love of God is different than the rest.

If you're a believer, a follower of Christ, then His love is in you, and you don't have to go looking for it. The capacity to love others as Christ loves them is part of your spiritual DNA. He fills us with his love. And He expects us to do something with that love and in order to do that, we have to get "out there". It's pretty easy to love others in the safety and comfort of our home church, but God wants us—no, he *commands* us—to love others as we love ourselves.

Loving someone means caring for them and wanting the best for them. *"This is how we know what love is: Jesus Christ laid down his life for us. And we ought to lay down our lives for our brothers and sisters."* (1 John 3:16, NIV)

Ask God to place people in your path daily that you can love or bless. Ask Him to help you see them the way He does. Uncomfortable? Yes. Out of the ordinary? Sure. But try to lay down a small bit of your life for someone else by loving them with extraordinary love, the same way Christ did for you. Get outside where people need the genuine and real love of Jesus and help bring them inside.

Questions for Reflection:
1. What's the hardest part about taking God's love "out there" for you?
2. Is there someone in your life God has been encouraging you to share his love with?
3. What's a positive step you can take this Advent season towards taking God's love "out there" into the world around you?

DAY THIRTY-ONE
God's Gift of Love

By James R. Russom, DMin.
NBC Faculty Emeritus

John describes the love that God has for us as "lavish." *"How great is the love the Father has lavished on us, that we should be called children of God! And that is what we are!"* (1 John 3:1, NIV) Lavish. What a unique word. As an adjective it means "luxurious and extravagant." As a verb it means "to give or bestow in extreme measures." During Advent we are reminded that God loves us so much He gave His Son Jesus to die for our sins and give us eternal life. Today you have the opportunity to thank God for loving you in such an extreme measure. The Apostle Paul wrote: *"He who did not spare his own Son, but gave him up for us all—how will he not also, along with him, graciously give us all things?"* (Romans 8:32, NIV)

One of the joys of Christmas is giving gifts to family and friends. It is an expression of appreciation, and it reminds people that they are loved and valued.

John reminds us that God so loved the world that he gave His only Son. God loves and values you so much that He has adopted you and called you His child. John says, "and that is what we are!" You didn't earn it; you don't deserve it. God chose to love you because you were created by a Heavenly Father who loves everyone with an everlasting love. It is so much a part of his nature that John would write, *"God is love."* (1 John 4:8, NIV) This is grace. God loves us not on the basis of our merit, but according to our need.

Take time today to thank God for the love He has lavished on you. And remember, *"We love him who first loved us."* (1 John 4:19, NIV) This love we have received is not to be kept only for ourselves. Jesus commands us to love others with this lavish love. *"My command is this: love each other as I have loved you. Greater love has no one than this: to lay down one's life for one's friends."* (John 14:12-13, NIV)

You have received the greatest Christmas gift of all. Now let us "lay down" our busy schedules to be sure we are taking the time to give that love to others. What a wonderful gift we have been given. What a privilege to give that gift to others.

Questions for Reflection:

1. How can you take time today to thank God for the love he has lavished on you? How can you make time to share that love with someone else?
2. Sometimes it's hard not to relate to our heavenly Father in light of our relationships with our earthly parents. Are there ways you struggle to see God's love because of ways you didn't receive love from them?
3. Do you ever act like God's love is something you have to earn? Why?

POST-ADVENT: TWO DAYS BEFORE CHRISTMAS TO NEW YEAR'S EVE

Finishing up love moves us from Advent into Christmas, which in the Christian calendar lasts all the way up until January 6th, a day known as Epiphany on the Christian calendar when we celebrate the visit of the Magi.

Our devotional ends on December 31st, but the virtues we uphold especially during Advent and Christmas aren't limited to a single season on the calendar. Keep the hope of Christ's coming to bring the kingdom into our daily lives alive all year. Believe in the peace of a prince who rejects the methods of the powerful and shows us a better way on the first of August. Rejoice in the coming of the newborn king in the middle of March. Make every day on the calendar a day to rejoice in the love of Christ that fulfills our hopes and brings peace and goodwill into our hearts.

DAY THIRTY-TWO

Christmas a Humbug?

By Josh Wright

'"A merry Christmas, uncle! God save you!" cried a cheerful voice. It was the voice of Scrooge's nephew, who came upon him so quickly that this was his first intimation he had of his approach.

"Bah!" said Scrooge, "Humbug!"...

"Christmas a humbug, uncle!" said Scrooge's nephew. "You don't mean that, I am sure?"

"I do," said Scrooge... If I could work my will," said Scrooge indignantly, "every idiot who goes about with 'Merry Christmas' on his lips, should be boiled with his own pudding, and buried with a stake of holly through his heart. He should!"'

—*A Christmas Carol* by Charles Dickens

With the possible exception of an unpleasant or greedy person being called a "Scrooge," there is perhaps no phrase as synonymous in our minds with *A Christmas Carol* as "Bah! Humbug!" For a long time, I didn't know what a "humbug" was. I just assumed it was a generic old-timey word of dismissal like "*Phooey!*" "*Hogwash!*" or "*Balderdash!*" But once you know that "humbug" means "to deceive or to trick," this part of the story starts to make a lot more sense.

Scrooge's nephew Fred barges into the counting house and tells his uncle "Merry Christmas!" Scrooge shoots back that Merry Christmas is a lie we tell ourselves to make up for our own shortcomings, whether its demanding generosity he doesn't feel we've earned or indulging in wasteful luxuries like lavish meals and extravagant gifts when we don't even have the money to pay our bills. Maybe for you instead the "trick" of Christmas is going out of our way to be charitable and kind for one month a year, when instead we should be seeking to live with that hope and joy in our hearts all year long. Or maybe it's getting so caught up in the decorations, the ribbons, and the presents that you lose sight of what really matters.

Scrooge's defense is half-hearted at best and rooted in his own greed and disdain for frivolity, but that doesn't mean his objection doesn't carry with it a kernel of truth, especially in the way we commercialize and trivialize a holiday that ought to mean so much more. Don't let the trappings and shiny lights blind you to the bigger task of compassion and kindness that are with us all throughout the year.

Questions for Reflection:

1. Are there any ways in your life you can think of where you've let Christmas become

a "humbug"? What can you do to change that this year?
2. Who needs to know from you that they have your compassion and kindness this season?

DAY THIRTY-THREE

Sacred Stew and Cornbread

By Jennifer Bergland

But the angel said to them, 'Do not be afraid; for see—I am bringing you good news of great joy for all the people: to you is born this day in the city of David a Savior, who is the Messiah, the Lord.'

(Luke 2:10-11, NRSV)

One of the things I love most about Christmas is the variety of traditions that develop over time. Growing up, my immediate family had our own traditions. We would attend our church's Christmas Eve service together. And, since my extended family didn't usually arrive until Christmas morning, after the service we'd head home for a quiet evening of homemade stew and cornbread. It became a sacred time for us, a chance to slow down and reflect on the meaning of Christmas before the controlled chaos of Christmas Day arrived.

As peaceful as those moments were, that first Christmas Eve was anything but quiet. Luke paints a vivid picture of how the angel's announcement broke the stillness with singing and a great heavenly host. The angel declared that something life-changing had happened: the long-awaited Messiah had come! Can you imagine being a shepherd on that hillside, hearing this proclamation for the first time? After centuries of waiting, the moment finally arrived—and it was declared with a heavenly broadcast of "good news of great joy for all people."

The anticipation that had been building for generations was finally fulfilled, and this wasn't just good news for a select few. The angel's words are clear: this joy is for everyone. That includes you and me; right here, right now. Christmas Eve carries its own kind of anticipation. For many, it's a time to prepare for the festivities of Christmas Day, a time filled with last-minute wrapping, cooking, and arranging. But in the midst of the busyness, we're invited to pause and remember the true reason for the whole celebration. It's more than the gifts, the food, or the gatherings—it's the joy of knowing that Christ, the Messiah, has come into the world.

This gift of Jesus is at the heart of everything we celebrate. So, while the world around us may be busy, let's carve out a moment to reflect. Why do we gather? Why do we give gifts? Why do we celebrate? It's because Christ, our Savior, has come! And that is the greatest news, not just for Christmas, but for all of our days.

Let the joy of Christ's love fill your heart tonight and lead you into the celebration of Christmas Day with gratitude and wonder.

Questions for Reflection:

1. Are there Christmas traditions you celebrate with your family that feel like sacred moments?
2. What are you most grateful for this Christmas? What are you struggling to feel grateful for?
3. As you prepare for this Christmas, take time to reflect on what Christ has done for you and how it motivates the joy of the holiday's celebrations.

DAY THIRTY-FOUR

A Star and a Promise

By Kylee Lane

In 2020, I had the privilege of seeing the Christmas star in the sky. As I held my precious 2-month-old that cold December night, I felt l had a greater appreciation for the Christmas story. As we all know, 2020 was full of uncertainty and confusion. In the middle of it all, my little family had begun some major life changes. My husband and I were moving from Missouri to Oklahoma, and I was about to give birth to our first baby. We gathered up our life, packed it into two moving trucks, and drove 6 hours to our new home (a house we had never seen in person). All the while I was in my third trimester, rushing to find a doctor and praying I would be a good mom.

As we gazed up at that star in the sky, I began to draw parallels between our journey that year and the

Christmas story. Mary was traveling while pregnant, facing the uncertainty of what was to come. She had just dealt with the judgment of those in her hometown. Leaving all that behind, she was facing the daunting task of being a first-time mom like me. But even though my story had some similarities with Mary's, I can't imagine what she went through: traveling to Bethlehem on a donkey, giving birth in a stable surrounded by animals, and the weight of holding the savior of the world in her arms.

The love I feel for my children is all-consuming. The pain, the tears, the sleepless nights; none of them matter every time I look at their little faces. I realize Mary must have felt the same way. And if that's the case, then how much more deeply must God feel the love He has for every one of His children.

> *"'For the mountains may move*
> *and the hills disappear,*
> *but even then my faithful love for you will remain.*
> *My covenant of blessing will never be broken,'*
> *says the Lord, who has mercy on you."*
>
> (Isaiah 54:10, NLT)

I am so thankful for the opportunity to be a mom, and to be loved with such abundance by our Creator.

Questions for Reflection:

1. What do you think about when you look up at the night sky? Spend some time today marveling at the majesty of God's creation.
2. Have you ever had to pack up your entire life and move away from everyone you knew? How did you see God at work in that move?
3. On this Christmas Day, celebrate the birth of the Christ child and rejoice in the great and wondrous love God possesses for all his children.

DAY THIRTY-FIVE

__Boxing Day__

By Josh Wright

Every year, my department at work takes part in our company's practice of "adopting" a family. We take up a donation and use that money and money the hospital provides to buy Christmas presents for the children of the family we "adopt." Too often, poverty means having to choose between joy and survival, and at Christmas everyone, rich or poor, should be able to rejoice in the generosity and merriment of the season.

For Canada, Australia, the UK, and other countries influenced by British culture, Boxing Day is a holiday that immediately follows Christmas. Though it has become more associated with after-Christmas sales and sporting events in recent years, the origins of the day go back almost 800 years and

began with the giving of gifts to the poor. The 26th of December is also celebrated as The Feast of St. Stephen, a holiday with similar concerns.

Boxing Day is traditionally associated with the wealthy giving gifts to their servants and churches opening up their alms boxes that have been collecting gifts for the poor all year and distributing them. It's a reminder of God's special concern for the poor and how Christ himself declared:

> *"The Spirit of the Lord is upon me,*
> *because he has anointed me*
> *to bring good news to the poor.*
> *He has sent me to proclaim release to the captives*
> *and recovery of sight to the blind,*
> *to let the oppressed go free,*
> *to proclaim the year of the Lord's favor."*
>
> (Luke 4:18-19, NRSV)

Boxing Day reminds us of the spirit of the season. Christmas is a time of open-handedness and special concern for the poor and needy among us. As we celebrate the one who came to proclaim peace on earth and goodwill to all of humanity, we remember his desire to lift up the downtrodden and oppressed. This is especially true for those of us who have been blessed with the means and resources to be generous.

Questions for Reflection:

1. What is something you do during the

Christmas season to show special concern for the poor? If nothing comes to mind, what's a new tradition you can start this year to help take care of the less fortunate?
2. When Jesus talked about "proclaiming the year of the Lord's favor," he was talking about Jubilee, a practice from the law of forgiving debts. We have no record of it ever having actually been carried out in the lives of Ancient Israel. What is something you can do in your life to live out the practice in the Lord's prayer of "forgiving your debtors?"
3. In the same way Christ was anointed to be about the work of reconciliation, God calls each of us to a purpose and a role for his kingdom's sake. If you're unsure what *your* calling might be, take time to pray and reflect on it now.

DAY THIRTY-SIX

Christmas for All

By Patrick Moore

Common themes are celebrated this time of year:
Gathering with family and friends
renewing relationships
Shining lights in the darkness, giving
hope to the hopeless
Generous giving as expressions of
love and valuing others
Wishing peace, hope, love, and goodwill to ALL people

Yet, there is also a sense of three distinct holidays:
One Holy ~ One Worldly ~ One Magical
All three simultaneously celebrated at once
Each distinctly and purely celebrated by some
The godly, the worldly, and the childlike

But none are as godly as the One who came as a child
None are purely worldly for all are God's creations
Created in his image and containing His breath
Even the jaded feel childlike awe from a heartfelt gift

Most celebrate a little of each in different proportions
The three intersect, intermingle, intermix, intertwine
They bump against each other and the edges blur
Complementing and contrasting
and synergizing together

The holy magical night God gifted
himself to us as a human child

The material rat race to find the perfect
gift for a special someone

The generous gift giving led by a mythical
version of a holy Saint

These three elements form the roots
of this dynamic holiday

The trunk is the merger of the holy, the
common, and the magical

Each of which are embodied in the
person of Jesus at his birth

Light and hope, family and friends,
Generosity and goodwill

These are the branches that spread
out into a beautiful tree

The tree of Christmas:

*Adorned with light, shining bright
hope into this dark season*

*Decorated with precious memories
collected throughout the years*

*Drawing in all people, like a lighthouse
beacon, into togetherness*

*Leaning on one another for support
in this time of great need*

*Providing light and warmth and hope
that greater light will return.*

*People who've been away seek out time
with family and friends.*

*People who never go to church go to candle
lit services and sing hymns.*

*People who don't believe in magic are
spellbound and enchanted.*

*People of all faiths are fascinated with the
wonder of the Christmas story.*

*Attended by Angels, Shepherds, and Astronomers,
God was never just the God of any one people group.
God is God of all whether acknowledged or not.
Abraham's offspring is a blessing to ALL nations.*

*Some try to claim and limit Christmas
to whom they choose.*

My God is not so small. He is the Lord of All.
All are chosen and invited by Him to celebrate His birth.
We choose how to respond. Christmas is for Everyone.

Questions for Reflection:

1. Christianity has a history of adopting and reinterpreting pagan practices, and some of that is definitely present in the ways we continue to celebrate Christmas. How do you feel about that?
2. Scripture tells us often that God is capable of working through unconventional means, often using people and places the Israelites wouldn't consider holy to accomplish holy purposes. Are there things in your life you've been too quick to judge as "not holy" God is trying to work through?
3. Despite Christmas Day almost certainly not having been the historical day Jesus was born, early Christians celebrated a "Christ mass" in the depths of winter for the same reason pagans had similar celebrations: to bring light and warmth into the cold and the darkness. Would you describe your current relationship with God as wintry? If not, have there been seasons of winter you've gone through in your faith?

DAY THIRTY-SEVEN

What Do I Have to Give?

By Aimee BoJack

While Jesus was in the Temple, he watched the rich people dropping their gifts in the collection box. Then a poor widow came by and dropped in two small coins. 'I tell you the truth,' Jesus said, 'this poor widow has given more than all the rest of them. For they have given a tiny part of their surplus, but she, poor as she is, has given everything she has.'

(Luke 21:1-4, NLT)

Have you ever skipped a party because you couldn't afford to get a gift? Or maybe you were worried what you had to give wouldn't really be appreciated?

We live in a world where big gifts are applauded,

and so did Jesus. But he wasn't impressed by the extravagance of the gifts being given by the rich in the temple that day. Jesus looked at this widow's sacrifice and appreciated the amount that it meant for the individual. The widow's mites clinked mightily in his ears, because he saw how much trust in God it took to let go of those coins.

In this season of cheerful giving, give cheerfully not because you feel pressured to do so, but out of the hope you place in your trust in God. What do you have to give? Let God work out the details of the time. He loved and appreciated the widow's might and cheerful faith more than the rich, who only gave what wouldn't be missed to impress other people.

What talents do you have? What time do you have that can be filled doing something for the sake of others? I ask that you pray about it wholeheartedly. We each have talents gifted to us by God to enrich the body of Christ. What talent is He wanting you to grow?

He has gifted us beyond measure. Let's be sure to give back to those around us all year long. As small as you think it is, it means the world to Him! It could be the one thing that reaches someone He has been calling without you even realizing it.

Mind if I pray with you for just a moment?

Heavenly Father, thank you for the gifts and talents You have given me. These talents and blessings are for Your glory. Help me see, know, and act on those talents and blessings as You see fit.

Questions for Reflection:

1. What are the first things that come to mind after praying those words?
2. Is there some way to give God has been guiding you to that you never thought of before? Are these perhaps things you have put off doing for any reason?
3. Is now the time God is urging you to act and grow what He has already planted in you?

DAY THIRTY-EIGHT

They Shall Call His Name Emmanuel

By Carole Liles

"Behold, a virgin shall be with child, and shall bring forth a son, and they shall call his name Emmanuel, which being interpreted is, God with us."

(Matthew 1:23, KJV)

The scriptures we read, the songs we sing, the greetings we send during the season of Advent resound with the beautiful names of Jesus. Messiah, Lamb of God, Prince of Peace, Savior...just to name a few. Emmanuel is the one that resonates the most in my heart.

Emmanuel translates to "God with us". Certainly,

God was with Adam in the garden and after, with Abraham as he waited on God's promise, with the despairing Israelites in the desert, with David in his remorse, with Hosea bringing Gomer back, with Jeremiah in the cistern, with the three Hebrews in the furnace, and with Mary telling Joseph she was with child: a child that was the Son of the Most High. He continued to be present with Peter, John, Paul, and Timothy.

As I look over my life, I see Emmanuel has been with me: on journeys of waiting, in the depths, through the frustrations, dangers, and persecutions. He has been with me through all the joys, triumphs, and everyday times as well. Emmanuel has always been walking beside me in the form of the Comforter, the Holy Spirit.

As I continue to read these accounts in the Bible, I see something else. The Patriarchs, the prophets, and the apostles all followed God. He was with them as they followed Him in their ups and downs, in the twists and turns of a fallen world, and in the miracles they experienced.

My attitude so often is that I expect Jesus to follow me around when I use my own wisdom, allowing fear and pride to drive me. Psalm 139:7 (NIV) says, *"Where can I go from your Spirit? Where can I flee from your presence?"* Yes. He is with me wherever I go.

Scripture also says in Matthew 9:9 (NIV), *"As Jesus went on from there, he saw a man named Matthew sitting at the tax collector's booth. 'Follow me,' he told him, and Matthew got up and followed him."* He was hated and despised by his fellow Jews, yet he put away his fear and pride and followed Jesus. I am called to follow as well. And he will be with me.

Jesus, our Emmanuel, came to be here with us and to show us the way. We follow Him to know the way to God and how to love our neighbors. The disciples had so little to go on when they left their lives to follow Emmanuel. On the other hand, in 2024 I have more evidence, more opportunities, more freedom, and fellow followers.

Emmanuel. God with ME. Right now. How can I not then lay down my life to follow Him?

Questions for Reflection:
1. Are there times in your life you feel as though you've expected God to follow you and not the other way around? How might those experiences have been different if you'd chosen to follow in the direction God wanted to lead?
2. What name for Christ resonates most with you? Reflect on that name and why it has

special significance in your heart.
3. Is there a direction God has been trying to lead you lately you've been hesitant to follow? Reflect and pray for God's guidance and the courage to follow wherever he might lead.

DAY THIRTY-NINE

A Sword Will Pierce Your Soul

By Josh Wright

In December of 2015 my life changed forever—my wife gave birth to our first child. Friends, family, and various other acquaintances tried to tell us how much our lives would change. I nodded politely, hearing them but not listening. I thought I understood it would be an adjustment. Babies change things, after all: routines, priorities, and your lifestyle in general. What I didn't understand was the sword that would pierce my soul.

When Jesus' parents went to the Temple to have him circumcised on the eighth day, they met Simeon. Simeon yearned for the reconciliation of Israel, and was guided to Mary, Joseph, and baby Jesus by the Holy Spirit. Since it had been revealed to Simeon that he would not die before he saw the Messiah, when he saw Jesus he took the baby into his arms and said:

*"Master, now you are dismissing your servant in peace,
according to your word;
for my eyes have seen your salvation,
which you have prepared in the presence of all peoples,
a light for revelation to the Gentiles
and for glory to your people Israel."*

(Luke 2:29-32, NRSV)

If that was where the encounter ended, it would be a nice, sweet story. Here is a righteous man who longs for the culmination of God's work through Israel, and now that he has seen it, he thanks God for the peace it has instilled in him. But, Simeon continues, and the words he speaks to Mary carry an altogether more sinister tone: *"This child is destined for the falling and the rising of many in Israel, and to be a sign that will be opposed so that the inner thoughts of many will be revealed—and a sword will pierce your own soul too."* (Luke 2:34b-35, NRSV)

I was in the hospital with my wife and son from Monday to Friday the week he was born, and I rarely left their side. But, on one of the rare occasions that I did leave the room, I received a text message from my wife that simply said, "Come back." I panicked. I rushed back to the room, with every possible worst-case scenario running through my brain. By the time I got back to the maternity ward, I was all but convinced that my wife and child were dead. But, when I got to the room, they were both fine. He was fussy, and she needed help. After we calmed him down, I spent several minutes crying, hands trembling. And Simeon's words about the sword came to mind.

That second word from Simeon is usually understood to be in reference to Jesus' ministry and passion narrative. That afternoon in the hospital, I discovered another meaning: to have a child is to have a sword stabbed into the core of who you are. And every time that child hurts, every time you're worried about their safety, the sword twists.

You never realize how helpless newborns are until you spend all day with one. There was a time when the Savior of the world couldn't support the weight of his own head. There was a time when the Prince of Peace couldn't be trusted to sleep without smothering himself. There was a time when The Great I AM, by whom and through whom everything was made, was unable to do anything at all for himself.

In all likelihood, there were times when his mother cried because he wouldn't eat. There were times when his father's heart stopped because he took a second too long to breathe. A sword pierced their souls, and the world was never the same.

Questions for Reflection:

1. What do you think it would have been like for Simeon, waiting in the Temple, day by day, growing older, year by year, hoping for

the day to come when he would see the Messiah?

2. C.S. Lewis said in *The Four Loves*, "to love at all is to be vulnerable. Love anything, and your heart will certainly be wrung and possibly be broken." What is it about love that makes all the potential for pain worth the risk?

3. All parents feel anxiety and get overwhelmed about the safety of their children. Imagine what that must have been like for Mary and Joseph, knowing they were raising the Messiah.

DAY FORTY

The Gift That Keeps on Giving

By James R. Russom, DMin.
NBC Faculty Emeritus

We have celebrated Advent and moved into the Christmas season. The miracle of love that God Himself provided when Jesus took on flesh, dwelled among us, and provided salvation for all humankind as the "Lamb of God that takes away the sin of the world." The good news of the Gospel is that anyone who believes on the name of the only begotten Son of God will be forgiven of their sins.

Matthew's Gospel presents Jesus as the Messiah who fulfilled prophecy by his birth, ministry, life, death, and resurrection. If we truly understand the meaning of Christmas, we realize that Christmas does not end on December 26th! The Christmas story began long before the Christ Child was born and will continue from now throughout eternity. It is the gift that keeps on giving.

The prophet Isaiah gives us the birth announcement...a child is coming. Imagine for a moment the joy of a young couple who discover their first child will soon be born. Matthew gives us the details of the birth event. This birth will be a miracle of God through the ministry of the Holy Spirit. Mary and Joseph are challenged by God's call for them to parent the Christ. They responded in trust, faith, and obedience, allowing them to participate in the greatest miracle of all time. Their example reminds us of how we are to live out this miracle in our own lives.

John reminds us of why Jesus came and what would be accomplished by his ministry and his sacrifice. *"The next day John saw Jesus coming toward him and said, 'Look, the Lamb of God, who takes away the sin of the world!'"* (John 1:29, NIV) The gift we received from God is not something to be celebrated once a year, but every day for the rest of our lives.

Jesus came that we might have life abundant: free and eternal. The redeeming grace of God is at work throughout the world seeking to save all who call upon the name of Jesus. Praise God for His eternal love and grace! We are saved because God gave us His Son as the Lamb of God who takes away our sins. But there is more: John the Baptist tells us Jesus will baptize us with the Holy Spirit!

Rejoice! The gift you received is alive and active. It is leading, guiding, directing, and empowering you to live the life God created you to live. Share the Good News with others and let them know that Christmas is more than an event...it is a way of life! Share the Gospel with others and give them access to the gift that keeps on giving.

Questions for Reflection:
1. What does it mean to you for Jesus to be the "lamb of God who takes away the sin of the world?"
2. What can you do to keep Christmas alive in your heart all year, not just during the "Christmas season?"
3. Does your life feel abundant right now? What is God wanting to do through you to make it abundant, or even more abundant?

ACKNOWLEDGEMENT

We are indebted to all the contributors who helped make this devotional a reality. Our deepest thanks to all our authors and all of our readers as well. Special thanks to Mitchell Murrow for his work on the cover design and Josh Wright for his work in envisioning this project, finding authors to participate, and doing the work of compiling and editing this volume.

ABOUT THE AUTHOR

Metroplex Church Of The Nazarene

Metroplex Church of the Nazarene is on the northwest side of Oklahoma City and started as a merger of Meridian Park Church of the Nazarene and Community Church of the Nazarene in 1984. We would love for you to be a part of our faith community, or just come visit to experience God's movement in our midst. See our website at https://www.metronazokc.org/ for more details about our location and service times.

Made in the USA
Coppell, TX
30 November 2024